Dedication

Once again I would like to dedicate this to absolutely everybody who was involved in its creation because they were involved with me.

In particular my new "mews," who I believe knows who he is.

Kitten

A Bird In The Hand…

I want more but I
Am so afraid of losing
What I have right now…

Please Be Patient With Me...

I'm on a new road
And I like the scenery.
I hope I get LOST…

What Is Love?

What, exactly, is Love?

Can you see it?
Is it really what you see in people's eyes when they look at each other or is that just physical? Do you notice when someone is showing it to you if you are not looking for it?

Can you hear it?
Many people have written poems and songs about what Love has and doesn't have… and yet they are all different.

Can you feel it?
Some people put so much weight on the word it becomes an anvil, crushing the target. Some people take it so lightly it becomes a helium balloon, floating endlessly away from the one trying to catch it.

Can you smell it?
I have seen people who close their eyes when they are near someone as if they smell their favorite meal. I have seen a look cross a guys face as if the thought of me liking him was as gross as smelling garbage.

Can you taste it?
What does it taste like; a bland vegetable that is "good for you" or a rich dessert?

I think Love is a lifelong piece of Art which is framed by a love for yourself and filled in by the love you show others.

Giving

It seems all I do is give.

When you ask me how my day was, I give.
You laugh with your friends about it later.

When you ask me to do something, I give.
You just don't want to do it yourself.

Need someone to switch shifts? I give.
When I need the same you can't help.

I get told to leave early so I don't have overtime.
I give.

I don't want to be, or even come off as, a stalker.
I give you space.

Like a stray cat later found in a road, I am out of sight out of mind.
I give up.

Missing

It's easier not
To miss you if I know you
Are missing me too

To My Loyal Subjects

Out there, in the world, I am a Princess.

Idealistic to a fault, sheltered, shy…
Even thought I had found my Prince Charming guy
Turned out to be the wrong Fairy Tale
I'm not Snow White, although I may be pale

I am more like Sleeping Beauty
Looking back at what happened to me
Under a sleeping spell for many years
Of bad self-esteem, overtaken by my fears

Only expressing my thoughts in fictional crushes
Telling myself that those pitiful rushes
Were what Love felt like and never showing
My feelings because they were not flowing

Up here, on this stage, I am Queen.

Much more realistic, open and brave
F*** that living in a cave
Have a swarm of drones wrapped around my finger
On one or two my gaze may linger

Using words The Princess would never say
In the shining light of day
If needed to express the truth of my life
And keep myself from taking in the strife

A newly crowned poetic Diva
Wanna know how I will see ya?
Speak to me, seek me out
And if I don't respond right away don't pout

You think you got what it takes?
Hold on, put on the brakes
I can see right through the fakes
And I have no time for foolish flakes

To those of you who are sincere
Give my next few words your ear
If you continue to be loyal to me
It will be worth your time, you'll see

Grateful

There are no words to
Describe what we have and that
Simply takes my breath away

Time To Play

You are not really
Giving me an order you
Are saying "pick me!"

Child

Childishly you throw a tantrum and start to cry
Push your dreams away and yell "GOODBYE!"

Child-like you forget your sorrow
And tell your dreams "See you tomorrow."

My Mom

Do you believe in angels? I do, my mom is one.

I can just see her on the day she entered Heaven: perhaps met by her own mother so she could get closure and be taught "the ropes" of Eternal Life. I see her throwing a huge fit in frustration over the future of her "kids" even though my brother and I were both over 30 when she passed.

The time would come for her to go into the Throne Room of my heavenly Father and she would march right in saying:
"I want a battalion of Guardian Angels sent to watch my kids, but especially my daughter."
"I know your Faith was broken when you were very young, but fear not. I have already done that. Angela has always had someone, or a group of people, to watch over her."
"She's just so helpless: as weak and fragile as the kitten she claims to be, despite everything I tried."
"Do you not trust your teachings? Even a kitten grows into a strong, independent, affectionate creature, with the proper care. Here, let me show you something."

He would show her my future accomplishments and happiness, everything she ever wanted for me, but she'd still have one question.
"Ok... but why, in all of the images you have shown me, was she always alone? The thing she wanted most (that I couldn't give her) was a 'someone special.'"
"I didn't forget about that, let me point him out to you."

So my mom is still looking out for me
Every day I have to sort what I see
From what I am only inferring.
This of course has got me purring.
Sometimes this journey is really fun,
And when it's over I will be with my One.

Picking Up The Pieces

Sometimes, my heart hurts so much I want to tear it out.

I want to lock it in a freezer to numb it and throw away the key.

I want to take a sledgehammer to it and when it is in pieces take the biggest shard and…

No. I want to pounce and tear yours out with my teeth… How DARE you have peace when I DON'T. How DARE you have connection when I don't. How DARE you have happiness… when I don't.

Then I take a closer look. You are staring at the ground. There are busted pieces of something at your feet and I don't know if yours was just made of weaker material or if you just dropped it more often but I think it's YOUR heart.

You look at me and smile.

Holding back tears I get a broom.

A Fan Letter To Donatello

Dear Donatello,

Is purple your favorite color too?

I can relate to why you won't let anyone into your shell… the more you open up to people the more they back away or use the info against you, right?

I wish your brothers would stop picking on you, but they think they are showing you love in their own way.

I write poetry the way you practice martial arts; I bet if you wrote poetry it would be about the beauty of working machines (I am fond of gadgets myself).

Let me hang out with you; I love to watch you when you are thinking. Intelligence breeds compassion.

I promise not to interfere with any of your experiments, or push any buttons… I'll even buy pizza.

Angela

My Biggest Fear

I don't ever want
To do anything to make you
Keep away from me

Your Poem

I keep your poem in my pocket.
I'd keep your picture in my locket,
If I hadn't had to hock it.

I keep your voice in my ears.
It helps quell my fears,
And sometimes keeps me from tears.

I keep your face in my mind.
You are always so kind,
A rare thing to find.

I keep your attention in my heart.
That helps it not to smart
Every time we have to part.

The Magic Is Mine

I see the grace of a kitten playing with its littermates and its toys
I ask it how I could become that graceful
It says "the magic is mine."

I see the beauty of a couple kissing under a full moon
I ask them how I could become that beautiful
They both say "the magic is mine."

I see the popularity of people I admire
I ask them how I can become popular
They each say "the magic is mine."

I see you listening to me ramble about what I have been through
You ask me how you can become so strong
I say "the magic is mine."

Where Is My Heart?

I don't think I picked
Up my heart last time I dropped
It… I think you did.

Flirtation

Flirting's not as fun
When the one you want to hear
From is not playing.

I Can Only Be Me

I can only be Me.

As much as I might wish to be "beautiful"
I'm not a foot taller
I'm not 10lbs lighter (always 10 more...)
I'm not blond over blue
I'm not a double D
I'm not that California look guys seem to like the most.
It's a stereotype, anyway.

As much as I might wish to be in a Broadway show
I'm not a dancer
I'm not a singer
I don't live in New York (I would hate it)
There are Tony awards for plays too though...

I tend to overanalyze things
It comes from years of locking my self in my own mind with only it for
company
I have always been more book smart than street smart
Always the little sister;
Sometimes getting treated like mom forced you to let me tag along
Sometimes being doted on like it's my birthday, when it's not.

All that I have is a (mostly) positive personality
Genuine friendliness
Thoughtful compassion
And admit it; my laugh may be loud but it is joyful and contagious

On the outside you may think I'm an ugly duckling, but...
If you let me, I can show you I am really a swan

Addicted

Wake, depressed, groan, kick
Think, shit, need, fix

Move, eat, don't, care
Think, you, not, there

Leave, house, start, work
Think, customer, fucking, jerk

On, computer, no, e-mail
Think, world, go, hell

Write, down, find, words
Think, stop, being, absurd

Calm, down, look, see
Think, want, stalk, me?

Poetry, reading, next, night
Think, you, there, right?

Sit, down, breathe, in
Think, watch, it, begin

Hear, see, laugh, rhyme
Think, more, next, time

Out Of Sync

I'm either too far
Ahead or too far behind
What am I missing?

From A To Z

You're just another letter in my alphabet...

A is for Angela, and I must say
Being true to my self is a test everyday
Can it be that my dreams are really so crazy?
Dreaming too much, am I just being lazy?

Everyone knows I am easily read
Fighting the thoughts inside of my head
Giving more, sometimes, than I should
Happiness, sometimes, being only a hood

Imagining places to run and hide
Just because I am hurting inside
Kindness naturally flowing from me
Letting people take easily

My defenses are down
No one else is around
Off to my domain I retreat
Proud of not giving in to defeat

Queen at least of my dreams
Regal, noble and more than she seems
Searching for connection
To give me direction

Under which guidance I have found
Valuable encouragement will abound
Winding from you to me and me to you
Xanthippe-like things I would never do

You're the one who makes my heart leap
And as for Zs... I won't be asleep.

Meaning

It is one thing to
Respond... it is another
To reciprocate.

Ode To An Open Mic

I just saw you.

You intrigued me, so I started to approach you. One of my friends was
standing nearby and I asked her "who is that?"
She told me your name and I continued on my way, each step making my
stomach flutter.

At last I was standing in front of you... I couldn't breathe until you spoke
first, asking my name.
I found enough of my voice to say it aloud and you started asking me
questions; not in an interrogation sort of way, but like you cared.
This threw me at first. I am used to people "humoring" me.
You didn't have the same vibe as all of the rest; the longer I talked with you
(and it was WITH you, not just TO you) the more I wanted to say. The more
I wanted to learn.

You have become ingrained in my life; you are part of my thought process,
you are my inspiration, you are my connection to my true self... I didn't
even know I was disconnected.
My mind has a new favorite game; it's called "what if..."

I can't wait to see you again.

Missing Pieces

My loneliness is like a deserted street on an October night; the kind that they use in slasher flicks.
When I think of that it makes me glad I am so invisible.

I mean, really, who wants to be the dazzling blond bimbo who runs around aimlessly screaming her head off because she just watched her attractive boyfriend get slaughtered just to run right into the killer?

Please.

A masochistic voice in my head pipes up with "at least they get attention."
So I sell my convictions for an invitation to your Halloween party.

This may sound clingy to you.
It is most likely NOT something you want to hear me go on about, but…
Guess what? It is a part of who I am.

I have a past just like you.
I am a jigsaw puzzle just like you.
I have been broken into pieces. Just like you.

The only question is: Do you have the rest of my pieces?

When I Close My Eyes

When I close my eyes I lose control.
My thoughts swirl like tornados taking me wherever they want.

Sometimes it is a bumpy, sickening ride through nightmares:
My mind decides to bring up every loss, every failure, and every
confrontation; taunting me with the promise of resolution only to have
something else go wrong.
Every voice that ever spoke against me blending with images from my
imagination.
I wake up unfulfilled.

Other times it is a stormy ride through fantasy;
My mind remembers every good time I have had or ever imagined; taunting
me with the promise of satisfaction only to snatch it away.
Every word I wish was said to me blending with images from my
imagination.
I wake up unfulfilled.

When I do open my eyes I can't get rid of the remnants of the dreams.
They effect every decision I make, taunting me with 'what ifs,' causing me
to take things too hard.
Everything I do or say blending with images from my imagination.
I live unfulfilled.

The only place I feel fulfilled is up here.
Hit or miss every word, every thought, every action is truly my own.
I feel the strength I wish I had, the certainty I wish I had, the joy I wish I had
all of the time.
This I control, and that's how I can deal with everything else long enough to
close my eyes.

When Dreams Expire

Here I sit, in front of this screen
Trying to remember my entire dream

It floats across my memory in bits and pieces
But parts are hidden in the creases

They don't show up on the screen behind my eyes
And that almost makes me want to cry

Where do dreams go when they expire?
Are they completely destroyed as if in a fire?

Or do they just get stored away
Brought back out another day?

And if so what good does that do
When the circumstances needed to achieve them are through?

Do they get to belong to someone else? Somewhere?
That doesn't seem in the least bit fair…

Then again, if the dream is not for me
My own dream I will someday see.

Hopefully.

Fooling The World

I wonder if they
Are watching us go back and
Forth like Grant and Karr

MY Siren Song

I like to watch your reaction to me
I can tell you've got it bad
If I saw that behavior in anyone else
I might even think it was sad

On you though it looks cute
Sometimes even hot
As if you were in a suit,
Or as if you're NOT…

You always know
Just what to do
And what not to show
Too soon

Like plans and smiles
And every little gift
Claiming that my feminine wiles
Could make tectonic plates shift

I will make you shout.
Mine's the best siren song you'll ever hear.
All you have to do is let me out
Of this side of the mirror.

My Man Poetry

Ok, so I can finally see
I have to introduce you to my man Poetry
He treats me better than men in my life or at work
(Not that any of them act like a jerk)
I'm just tired of playing these games
And so I tell you, without naming names
It's all just pretend when they talk to me
And the ones I thought were real, well, I've gotten strike 3
So if you are asking if you're guy #4
Know that I am looking for a whole lot more
Or maybe it's less, because all I want really
Is for someone to want to get to know me
I'm so sick of being in friendships alone
Yet I'm not going to just hide out at home…

At least not all the time.

Life Goes On

I breathe in the cool fall air
Life goes on
I feel the cold breeze blow through my hair
Life goes on

Like the leaves I want to blow away
Life goes on
Please don't make me deal with this sadness today
Life goes on

I'm not used to not sleeping at night
Life goes on
Something is not completely right
Life goes on

Too many things on my mind
Life goes on
Including notions I must leave behind
Life goes on

They have to go to make room for new growth
Life goes on

I wish it was Spring again.

www.ingramcontent.com/pod-product-compliance
Lightning Source LLC
Chambersburg PA
CBHW030009040426
42337CB00012BA/716